DATE DUE

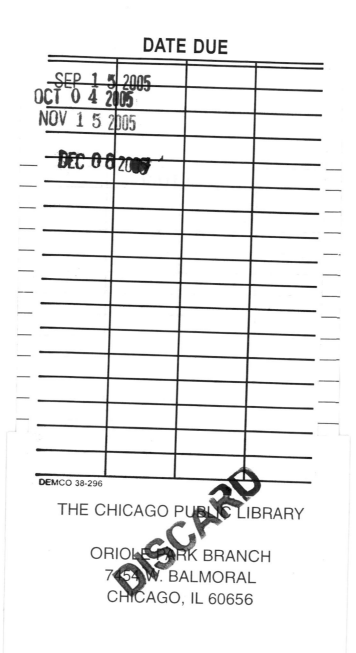

SEP 1 5 2005			
OCT 0 4 2005			
NOV 1 5 2005			
DEC 0 6 2005			

DEMCO 38-296

Explore Your Senses

TASTE

by Laurence Pringle

BENCHMARK BOOKS

MARSHALL CAVENDISH
NEW YORK

The author wishes to thank Dr. Edward J. Kormondy, Chancellor and Professor of Biology (retired), University of Hawaii-Hilo/West Oahu for his careful reading of this text and his thoughtful and useful comments. The text has been improved by Dr. Kormondy's notes, however the author assumes full responsibility for the substance of the work, including any errors that may appear.

Benchmark Books
Marshall Cavendish Corporation
99 White Plains Road
Tarrytown, NY 10591

Text copyright © 2000 by Laurence Pringle
Medical illustrations copyright © 2000 by Marie T. Dauenheimer, CMI
Pringle, Laurence P.
Taste / by Laurence Pringle.
p. cm. — (Explore your senses)
Includes bibliographical references and index.
Summary: Describes the parts of the mouth and how they function and discusses why things taste different to different people, the relationship between smell and taste, the sense of taste in animals, and more.
ISBN 0-7614-0736-7
1. Taste—Juvenile literature. [1. Taste. 2. Mouth. 3. Senses and sensation.]
I. Title. II. Series: Pringle, Laurence P. Explore your senses.
QP456.P75   1999   612.8'7—dc 21   98-28042   CIP   AC

Printed in Hong Kong

6   5   4   3

Photo research by Linda Sykes Picture Research, Hilton Head, SC

Cover photo: Stock Boston / Jeffry W. Myers
Picture credits: The photographs in this book are used by permission and through the courtesy of: Photo Edit: 4 (bottom), Jonathan Novaos; 11 (right) Felicia Martinez; 15 David Young/Wolff. Photo Researchers: 4 (top) E. R. Degginger; 7 (top) Prof. A. Motta/Univ. La Sapienza, Rome; 13 (left) Day Williams; 14 Gordon Smith; 17 Marcello Bertinetti; 21 (right) USDA; 23 Y. Landeau/Jacana; 24 John Serrao; 25 (left); 25 (right) Ray Colemans; 26 C. Nardin/Jacana; 27 Steinart Aquarium; 29 (top) Peter Skinner; 29 (bottom) Carlos Golden/Science Photo Library. Stock/Boston: 21 (left) Sue Klemens. The Image Bank: 5 Mark/Es Product; 7 (bottom) A. Boccacco; 11 (left); 18 Nino Mascardi. Tony Stone Images: 13

Contents

"**Y**um."

"Delicious."

"Yuck!"

Even though there are just a few kinds of taste *receptors* in our mouths, we can experience a wonderful variety of flavors. Our sense of taste also enables us to detect bitter-tasting and possibly dangerous substances before we swallow them.

The human sense of taste is much simpler than our senses of sight, hearing, and smell. It is, in fact, tied in some ways to the sense of smell. What we call the flavor of a food or drink is partly its taste and partly its scent.

Tasting, however, is more complex than it was once thought to be. Scientists have studied the sense of taste in rats, catfish, mud puppies, and people. As a result, they have tossed out ideas about the sense of taste that were widely accepted until recently. They have also learned that some people are *supertasters*, with an especially keen sense of taste.

Are you a supertaster? In this book you can find out. You can also discover how your sense of taste works, and how it affects your life in surprising ways.

The mud puppy salamander, above, has very large taste buds. Studies of mud puppies have helped us understand how people sense all of the flavors in their lives.

Lean close to a well-lit mirror. Stick out your tongue and look at it. What do you observe?

Your tongue, and the whole inside of your mouth, is wet with a fluid called *saliva*. It contains *mucus*, a protective fluid that is given off by glands. It also contains an *enzyme*, a natural chemical that begins to digest the food and drink you put in your mouth. Saliva has another value. You could not detect the flavor of foods if the surface of your tongue and the rest of your mouth were not wet.

Your tongue, you'll notice, is not a smooth surface. It is covered with small bumps. It may even feel a little bumpy to your fingertip. The little bumps are called *papillae*.

Papillae come in different shapes. A close-up photograph of the tongue looks like a landscape of odd-shaped mountains. Some are flat-topped mounds surrounded by a trench. Some are mushroom shaped. Some look like leaves.

Just below the surface of each papilla are *taste buds*. The papillae shaped like mushrooms contain between one and five taste buds. The other kinds of papillae contain up to 250 taste buds. Although taste buds are concentrated on the tongue, they can also be found on the roof of your mouth and on the inside of your cheeks. Taste buds also occur on your *uvula*, the flap of flesh that dangles at the back of your mouth. In all there are several thousand taste

The tiny bumps on your tongue are called papillae. Here, drawn in a side view, are the three kinds. Each papilla contains one or many taste buds.

taste buds

taste buds

taste buds

Look at Your Tongue

buds in your mouth that are ready to help you experience all the flavors of the world.

The surface of the tongue, right, magnified 80 times, shows two kinds of papillae.

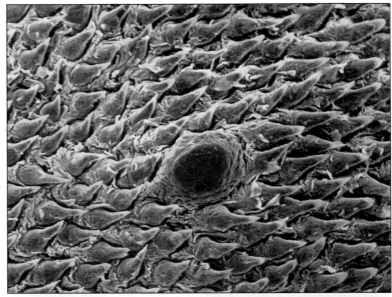

Taste buds were given their name because they look like microscopic flower buds. Each bud is hidden just beneath the surface of a papilla. It rests below a little opening, called a *pore*.

When microscopic *molecules* of food enter the pore of a taste bud, they come in contact with taste cells. Nerve fibers connect each taste cell with the brain, where the sensation of taste actually occurs. However, the sense of taste is not that simple. Taste cells are also connected to one another by nerve fibers. They exchange and combine taste information before it is sent on to the brain. Taste buds wear out and are replaced with fresh buds every week or two.

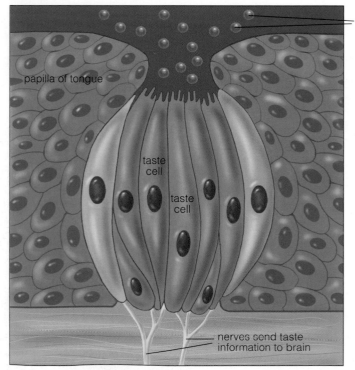

food molecules enter pore

papilla of tongue

taste cell

taste cell

nerves send taste information to brain

A taste bud

Taste Buds and Taste Cells

Think of all the different tastes you enjoy. In ice cream alone there are so many flavors. You might expect that there are hundreds or even thousands of different kinds of taste cells in the taste buds of your mouth. Actually, only five different taste cells are known, including one that was finally proved to exist in 1997.

The four basic tastes detected by taste buds are sweet, salty, sour, and bitter. The fifth is called *umami* (pronounced "ooo-mah-me"). A century ago a Japanese scientist gave the name umami to a taste he could not identify in seaweed. Now the actual taste cells that detect umami in food have been identified.

Umami is a hard-to-describe, savory flavor. It is the taste of a natural chemical called *glutamate*. Some people recognize it when a substance called monosodium glutamate is added to foods, particularly to Chinese foods. But glutamate is also naturally present in many other foods we eat.

Some scientists suspect that there may be a few other kinds of taste detectors in taste buds. One might detect the taste of fat, another the taste of a substance called *tannin* in tea. More study must be done to find out. There are still many mysteries about our sense of taste.

taste messages are sent to this part of the brain

Having a cold is no fun. Often it starts with a sore throat. Later, even though your throat feels better, you may have a runny nose. Mucus clogs your two *nasal cavities*. You may have trouble breathing through your nose. You may also have trouble smelling, and even tasting.

Your sense of taste is linked with your sense of smell. Most of what we call the flavor of food is a combination of its scent and its taste.

Even as you bring food close to your mouth, scent molecules rise up your nose. More scent molecules are released from food when you put it in your mouth. They rise up the *pharynx*, the passageway that connects the back of your mouth to the back of your nasal cavities. Scent detectors send messages to your brain about the food's smell at the same time taste detectors are sending messages to the brain about its taste. The flavor you taste is the result of both scent and taste.

When you have a cold, the thick mucus in your nose prevents the scent detectors there from working very well. But you don't have to have a cold to see how important a food's odor is to its flavor. Try this: get some jellybeans of different flavors—orange, licorice, strawberry, and so on. As you chew them—one at a time—notice how you can identify their distinctive tastes.

Spread a variety of jellybeans in front of you and

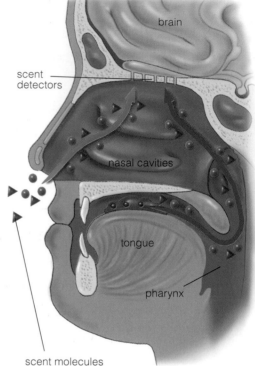

brain

scent detectors

nasal cavities

tongue

pharynx

scent molecules

Taste and Smell

close your eyes. With one hand, close your nostrils tightly so you cannot smell. With the other hand, pick a jellybean, put it in your mouth and chew it. Can you recognize its taste? Try this with other jellybeans.

You can try this with a friend, and also try a similar test with other kinds of foods. Cut an apple, pear, and raw potato into pieces of the same size. Usually people have no trouble telling these foods apart when they chew them. Blindfold a friend's eyes and test these foods, one at a time, while his or her nose is held tightly closed.

You will discover that it is hard to recognize the taste of food without using the sense of smell.

Can you identify jelly bean flavors, or tell apple, pear, and potato apart when you chew them but do not smell them?

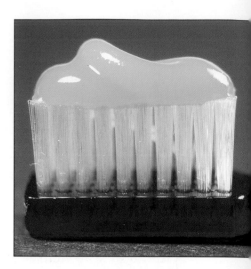

Orange juice tastes bitter if you drink it soon after brushing your teeth. Toothpastes contain a detergent that keeps taste buds from sensing sweetness for a while.

Many books that tell about the sense of taste show a map of the tongue. The map shows that different flavors are detected in different regions of the tongue. It shows that sweet things are sensed near the tip of the tongue. Other flavors are detected in other parts, with bitter tastes sensed near the back of the tongue.

Scientists who study the sense of taste now say this map is wrong. They discovered that a single taste bud can be sensitive to more than one taste. Even a single taste cell can respond to salt, sweet, sour, and bitter. Also, the tongue alone is not our only way to taste things. In rare accidents some people lose all or most of their tongue. Taste buds in other parts of their mouths still work, and they find they can still sense flavors fairly well.

Studies of how taste buds works have shown that taste cells are more sensitive to some flavors than others. When a spoonful of sugar is mixed into two hundred spoonfuls of water, taste cells can still detect the sweetness.

Taste cells are even more sensitive to other tastes. They are most sensitive to bitter tastes. Taste cells can usually detect a bitter taste even when one part of a bitter-tasting substance is diluted in 2,000,000 parts of water.

Food or drink that is poisonous often has a bitter taste. So being very sensitive to bitter tastes helps

Taste Buds at Work

protect humans from harm. This sensitivity was especially helpful thousands of years ago, when people were trying many kinds of plants and other foods for the very first time.

Most of the other basic tastes that people can detect also help people survive. A sweet taste usually signals a high-energy food. A salty taste signals a food that can replace salt lost by sweating when a person exercises or does hard physical work. A sour taste often signals that fruit is not ripe. Each taste gives important information about foods.

Sometimes it is possible to fool your taste buds. In Africa, a certain berry is sometimes called the miracle fruit. When people chew these berries, they can no longer taste anything sour. Instead, lemons, rhubarb, and other sour-tasting foods have a strong sweet flavor. Only after all of the bits of miracle fruit have been swallowed do sour-tasting foods have their normal flavor.

Lemons have a strong sour flavor, but they taste sweet after a person eats some African miracle fruit berries.

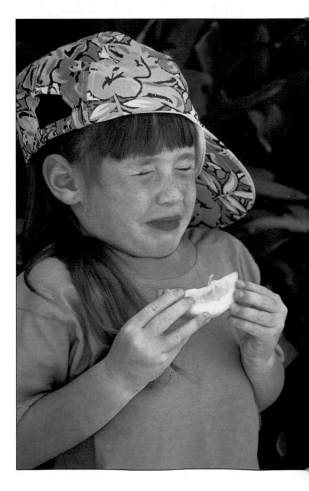

We say that some kinds of spicy foods taste hot, but there are no taste cells that detect hot things. Scientists have discovered that there is more to the flavor of food than its taste and its odor. A food's flavor also includes its temperature and even its ability to cause pain!

Besides taste buds, your mouth contains nerve cells, or neurons, that detect temperature, touch, and pain. These are the same kind of neurons that are all over the skin of your body. In your mouth and on your tongue, they send messages to your brain about foods and drinks.

When you drink soda, you feel a tingling sensation in your mouth. Tiny bubbles are bursting, and carbon dioxide gas is released from each bubble. It irritates the neurons that sense pain.

Some foods also stimulate pain receptors. They include chili peppers, ginger, horseradish, black pepper, mustard, and curry. Even though such foods cause some pain, many people like them for that very reason. In the United States, the popularity of spicy foods that irritate pain receptor cells is growing.

Neurons in your mouth also tell you about its temperature. Some foods just taste better after they have been heated. Temperature also seems to strengthen the flavor of certain tastes. When drinks are warmed they taste sweeter than cold drinks.

More Than Taste Buds

Sometimes, even the sound of a food as we eat it adds to our enjoyment. Food manufacturers know this. They know that people expect potato chips to give off a crisp, crackling sound as they are chewed. Potato chips contain countless little air pockets that make a crispy sound when we bite through them. Also, many potato chips are made so they are too big to fit into your mouth. With your mouth partway open, you hear the full crunchy sound when you bite into a chip.

Potato chips are deliberately made to be noisy food.

Enchiladas in red chili pepper sauce and other spicy food stimulate pain receptors in your mouth.

If you talk to your friends about foods they like, you will soon discover that not everyone agrees on taste. You may say "Yuck!" to a friend's favorite meal.

People live in different taste worlds. They do not experience the flavors of foods exactly the same way. Many factors affect how people respond to different tastes. One factor is age. The mouths of babies have more taste buds than adults. Also, babies are born with a desire for sweet tastes. This makes sense because the first food of human infants, and of other baby *mammals*, is milk. It contains milk sugar. Fruits and other foods that a young child needs for healthy growth also contain different kinds of sugar, and taste sweet.

As humans grow older they gradually lose their ability to taste the full flavors of food and drink. The number of taste receptors in their mouths decline. People who are seventy or more years old often say that many foods are bland, with very little flavor. Older people tend to put pepper or other strong-tasting ingredients on their foods to make them more tasty.

A person's family and culture also affect how he or she responds to different tastes. Young children in Mexico do not instantly

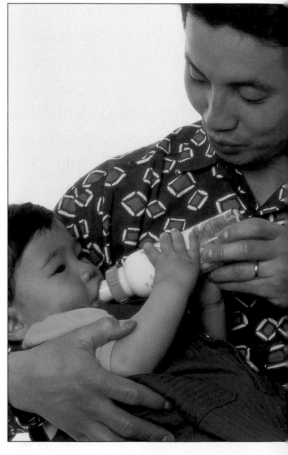

Infants crave sweet tastes—in milk, fruit, and other foods they need for good health.

in Different Taste Worlds

like chili peppers. They grow to enjoy them because hot-tasting foods are so commonly served in Mexico. Spicy curries are part of growing up in India. In your own family, you may be fond of some foods simply because they are often served, and you have learned to like the taste.

Parents affect their children's food likes and dislikes in another way. Just as people *inherit* eye color and the shape of their face from their parents, they also inherit their tasting ability.

This was discovered by accident in 1931. A chemist named Dr. Arthur Fox mixed some ingredients to form a compound he called PTC (for phenylthiocarbamide). Another chemist in his laboratory mentioned that PTC had a strong bitter taste. Dr. Fox tried it and tasted nothing.

Dr. Fox offered many people a taste of PTC crystals. Three out of every four people said that PTC was bitter tasting. The others could not taste it at all. Eventually scientists learned that people all over the world were either tasters or nontasters of PTC. More important, they learned that the ability to taste this substance was inherited. So is the ability to taste many other flavors.

Every culture has favorite foods. In this photo, Japanese boys enjoy octopus.

All people on Earth can be divided into three groups: regular or medium tasters, nontasters, and supertasters. The difference in their tasting ability lies in the number of taste buds in their mouths.

About half of all people are medium tasters. They have many taste buds, though not nearly as many as supertasters. They can taste all sorts of flavors. They enjoy a wide range of foods because most foods are not too sweet, sour, bitter, or salty.

About one out of four people are nontasters. They have very few taste buds, and a poor sense of taste. Blindfolded, nontasters often cannot tell the difference in taste between skim milk and heavy cream. Nontasters often use pepper and other strong-tasting seasonings in order to give their food a noticeable flavor.

Nontasters may have as few as eleven taste buds on a square centimeter of their tongue's surface. That's a square this size:

In contrast, supertasters may have as many as 1,100 taste buds in the same area. This makes supertasters highly sensitive to flavors. Their mouths are also more than sensitive to pain and heat than medium tasters.

As a result, supertasters find chili peppers, ginger, and other highly spicy foods unpleasant to eat. A bitter-tasting or sour-tasting food or drink is

Supertasters can detect slight differences in the amount of fat in milk. Nontasters cannot.

extremely bitter or sour to a supertaster. The caffeine in coffee tastes most bitter to a supertaster. Grapefruit juice and even orange juice may taste too sour to drink. To a supertaster, sweet tastes are also very strong. Cake frosting may taste sickeningly sweet.

Being especially sensitive to heat, supertasters often wait for hot foods to cool off. Supertasters are also very sensitive to fats. Some supertasters were given the same blindfolded test of several milk samples that were taken by nontasters. (The samples were: skimmed milk, 1 percent fat, 2 percent fat, 4 percent fat, half milk and half cream, and heavy cream.) As the fat content increased, supertasters could detect the change.

In another test, three groups of children who were known to be nontasters, medium tasters, or supertasters were given cheddar cheese. The non-tasters liked it best. Regular tasters liked it fairly well. The supertasting children disliked it because of a strong bitter taste. Cheddar cheese does have some ingredients that taste slightly bitter to regular tasters as well.

Just by reading this far you have some clues about whether you are a supertaster, a medium taster, or a nontaster. You can find out more by observing the papillae in an area near the tip of your tongue. Just follow the directions (right).

LOOK AT YOUR TONGUE
Look closely at the papillae near the front of your tongue. Gently push on them with your finger or toothbrush to get an idea of their size and numbers. Nontasters have large, scattered papillae. Supertasters have many very small, tightly packed papillae, Medium tasters do not have as many.

Of all supertasters identified so far, two out of three are females. Whether female or male, however, their sensitivity to flavors can have a strong influence on their lives.

Supertasters tend to avoid sugary and fatty foods throughout their lives. They usually have healthy diets. One study of a group of older women showed that the supertasters were thinner than nontasters. The supertasters also had lower amounts of a waxy substance called *cholesterol* in their blood. This made them less likely than others to die of heart disease.

Supertasters say that most alcoholic drinks taste bitter. They tend to be nondrinkers or drink only small amounts of *alcohol.* This also helps keep supertasters healthy.

On the other hand, supertasters avoid some healthy foods because they find the taste too strong or unpleasant. For example, broccoli has a strong bitter flavor to supertasters. This vegetable contains natural chemicals that help protect people from *cancer.* So do some other vegetables and fruits. There is concern that supertasters may increase their risk of getting cancer by avoiding foods that taste strongly sour or bitter. Fortunately there are ways to prepare broccoli and other healthy foods so supertasters find them good tasting.

Scientists are trying to learn more about both

Life as a Supertaster

supertasters and nontasters. They suspect that nontasters may also harm their health because of some of their food and drink choices. As we learn more, perhaps food manufacturers and restaurants will sell foods especially prepared for all of the nontasters and supertasters that, added together, make up half of the human population.

Foods that many people enjoy, such as candy and broccoli, may be unpleasantly sweet or bitter to a supertaster.

Many more women than men are supertasters. Scientists have tried to figure out why this is true. They believe it is more important for females to be supertasters because women are child bearers. Babies develop within their bodies. Whatever a woman eats or drinks also feeds the developing baby in her womb. So it is vital for women to be able to avoid food or drink that might be harmful. A woman's taste buds are a defense against harm to her baby. This may explain why more women than men are supertasters.

For all humans a bitter taste is a warning. Just as people have a natural liking for a sweet taste, they have a natural dislike for a bitter one. A bitter flavor warns of a food or drink that might be poisonous.

Supertasters say that bitter tastes are especially unpleasant. Scientists have found that women who are supertasters eventually become less sensitive to bitter tastes, but do so after they can no longer have babies. They have also discovered that women who are nontasters and medium tasters become more sensitive to bitter tastes during the first three months of pregnancy. For example, some women who liked coffee found it unpleasantly bitter after getting pregnant. Their sense of taste was at work, protecting the developing baby in their wombs from possible harm.

Of course, many foods with a bitter taste are not harmful. Broccoli and cauliflower are just two

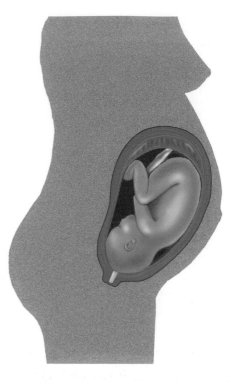

Anything a woman eats, drinks, or inhales can affect the well-being of a baby developing in her womb.

examples. Supertasters usually avoid them but other people do not. Besides, some people like to experience unusual flavors. Some are taste bud thrill seekers.

One food is potentially deadly, but is also considered to be a taste treat. Diners in Japan pay as much as $300 for a meal of this delicacy. It is *fugu*, the Japanese name for blowfish. The muscles of fugu are served raw, and have a faintly sweet taste.

The flesh is harmless. However, the skin, intestines, and some other parts of blowfish contain one of the most powerful poisons on Earth. In Japan, more than a hundred people used to die each year from eating fugu. Now specially trained fugu chefs take great care to separate the poisonous parts. Deaths from eating fugu are unusual these days, but fugu dinners are still a little risky.

Some Japanese people continue to dine on fugu. They seem to like both the taste and the risk.

Parts of fugu, blowfish, are deadly poison, while its flesh is considered a delicacy.

Throughout the animal world—from jellyfish to monkeys—bitter tastes are avoided. Many plants contain bitter-tasting substances that act as a defense against insects and other animals that might eat their leaves and stems.

One of the most common kinds of bitter-tasting chemicals in plants are the *alkaloids*. More than four thousand varieties are known. Alkaloids include caffeine in coffee, nicotine in tobacco, and a deadly poison called strychnine. Nicotine is also a poison that repels insects from tobacco leaves. The amount in a cigarette may be enough to kill an insect but is not enough to kill a person.

Another group of bitter-tasting plant chemicals are the *glycosides*. They are present in many plants, including foxglove and milkweed. The milkweed family of plants gets its name from a sticky white sap that flows through stems and leaf veins. A glycoside poison in the sap is bitter-tasting and poisonous.

Most plant-eating animals avoid milkweed. However, a few kinds of insects do eat the leaves. They include a kind of aphid, milkweed beetles, milkweed bugs, and the caterpillars of monarch butterflies. After eating milkweed, the insects contain some glycoside poison. These insects, including adult monarch butterflies, are marked with bright orange or red color. To birds and other creatures that might eat the insects, the color warns: "Beware! Poison!"

Warning Colors

Other creatures that have "Don't Eat Me!" warning colors include small tropical frogs. Most frogs have dull colors that help them hide from predators. Some little frogs of Central and South America are brightly colored, and they have poisonous skin. Their skin has a bitter taste, and the frogs are deadly if swallowed.

Some of these frogs produce their own poisons. However, at least one kind gets most of its poison from eating ants of the rain forest. The poison is an alkaloid, and the ants get it from plants they eat.

Orange or red insects, or brightly colored frogs, contain poisons. The poison dart frog, right, has poisonous skin because it eats bitter-tasting ants that have eaten bitter-tasting plants.

Many mammals have more taste buds than people. A supertasting person may have 10,000 taste buds, but a rabbit has 17,000, a cow 25,000. Like humans, all of these mammals have their sense of taste in their mouths. The same is true of birds, reptiles, and other land animals with backbones.

If you dip your toes in lemonade, or ice cream, or mashed potatoes, you will not taste a thing. However, some familiar insects taste with their feet. Other creatures, including earthworms, detect tastes with their whole bodies. They have simple taste receptors everywhere. The ones around their mouths are especially sensitive to sweet tastes. Earthworms can also detect an acid taste. This helps them avoid highly acidic soil that could be harmful.

Fish also have taste receptors on their bodies, as well as on their heads and lips. Their sense of taste is more sensitive than humans. They can detect a very faint sweet taste that is diluted in the water around them. Finding food by taste is especially important for fish that live in muddy waters or feed in the dark. Catfish have whiskerlike barbels covered with thousands of taste receptors.

Like many fishes, there are insects that have already tasted their food before it enters their mouths. Moths, butterflies, houseflies, and other insects often have taste receptors on their antennae and feet. A fly walking on your plate is actually tasting

An earthworm's body is covered with simple taste detectors.

The Taste Sense of Animals

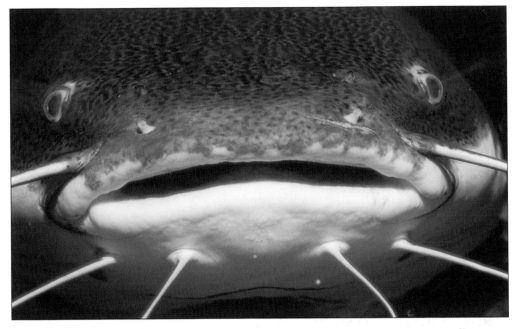

A catfish's barbels look like a cat's whiskers but actually help the fish taste food.

your food with receptors on the tiny hairs on its feet. A blowfly has three thousand of these hairs on its six legs.

Many insects are especially sensitive to sweet tastes—a sign that a food rich in energy has been found. On a butterfly, taste receptors are found on the tiny hairs near the tips of its back legs. A butterfly stepping around on a flower is tasting the blossom's nectar. If the nectar is sweet enough, the butterfly uncoils its sucking tube (proboscis) and drinks.

Each fall monarch butterflies fly hundreds or even thousands of miles. They spend the winter along the California coast or in central Mexico. Some monarchs actually gain weight on their long journey, pausing to sip sweet food from flowers that they have first tasted with their hind feet.

Of the human senses, the sense of taste is not nearly as important as sight, smell, and hearing. However, it does help protect us from eating spoiled or poisonous foods. It affects our food and drink choices. These choices can in turn affect our diet, weight, and health. And, of course, the sense of taste gives us the pleasure of a wonderful variety of flavors.

The sense of taste grows weaker with age, and that can't be helped. However, people young and old can protect their sense of taste from harm. The medical term for a sense of taste that is not working properly is *dysgeusia*.

One cause of dysgeusia is smoking. Anyone who wants to savor the full flavor of foods should never smoke tobacco. Smokers damage both their sense of taste and sense of smell.

Dysgeusia can also be caused by neglecting to brush and floss your teeth. This can lead to gum disease, and a more serious case of dysgeusia. Some kinds of medicines and drugs can also dull a person's sense of taste, or leave a metallic taste in the mouth.

Some patients who complained that all foods tasted awful were found to be lacking enough zinc in their saliva. Zinc is a metal that humans need for good health. Given some zinc pills, the patients soon were able to enjoy eating again.

Many cases of dysgeusia can be treated successfully. Damaged taste buds are soon replaced by fresh

Care of Your Sense of Taste

new ones. The sense of taste returns, and so do the delights of life's flavors. Delicious!

Smoking harms a person's ability to detect flavors and scents. By keeping teeth and gums healthy, people also help keep their sense of taste healthy.

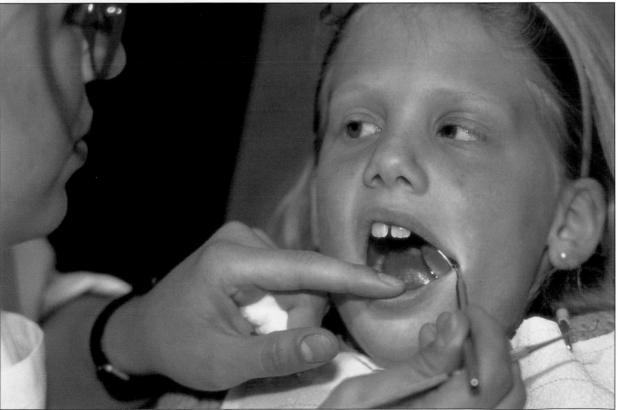

alcohol—a colorless liquid that is the world's most widely used drug. Ethanol alcohol, the kind used in drinks, may produce relaxed feelings when used in small amounts. Larger amounts cause drunkenness and even death.

alkaloids—bitter-tasting poisonous chemicals produced by plants that discourage insects and other animals from eating the plants. Thousands of alkaloids are known. One is nicotine, a poison in tobacco leaves.

cancer—a disorder in which cells grow wildly, producing growths called tumors. Many cancers can be treated successfully, but cancer is still the second-leading cause of human death in the United States.

cholesterol—a waxy substance produced within the human body and also present in meat, cheese, and other foods from animals. Excess cholesterol can clog arteries that carry blood and increase the risk of heart attack.

dysgeusia—the medical term for a faulty sense of taste.

enzymes—natural chemicals (proteins) in the body that are vital in the workings of an animal's organs. An enzyme in the mouth called ptyalin begins the process of digesting food.

fugu—the Japanese name for blowfish, which are able to inflate themselves as a defense against being swallowed by larger fish. The skin and internal organs of a blowfish contain enough poison to kill thirty people, but the flesh, which is harmless, is considered a delicacy.

glutamate—a natural chemical present in many foods that has a savory, meatlike flavor. In 1997 scientists discovered that humans have taste receptors in their mouths that are sensitive to the glutamate taste, which is also called umami.

glycosides—like alkaloids, glycosides are poisonous substances produced by plants that repel animals from eating the plants.

inherit—to acquire a characteristic from an ancestor through the genetics of reproduction. Everyone inherits their looks and many other characteristics from their parents, and also from their grandparents and earlier ancestors.

mammals—warm-blooded animals with backbones that nurse their young with milk.

molecule—the smallest possible amount of a substance that still has the chemical characteristics of that substance.

mucus—a sticky fluid given off by glands that protects surfaces within the body.

Glossary

nasal cavities—twin chambers, one for each nostril, through which inhaled air flows on its way to the lungs.

papillae—little bumps that cover the surface of the tongue (and are also found at the root of a hair and a developing tooth). There are several shapes of papillae. Tiny openings in the surface of papillae allow bits of food to reach taste buds.

pharynx—the passageway between the nasal cavities and the back of the mouth.

pore—a tiny opening. Molecules of food and drink pass through pores to reach the taste buds in the surface of papillae on your tongue.

PTC—a man-made chemical compound (phenylthiocarbamide) that tastes strongly bitter to most people but is tasteless to others. Research with PTC led to the discovery that people inherit some of their tasting ability from their parents.

receptor—a nerve cell that is sensitive to a stimulus. Taste receptors are sensitive to different flavors.

saliva—fluid in the mouth secreted by salivary glands. Saliva keeps the tongue and mouth surfaces moist, and contains the enzyme pytalin that begins the digestion of food.

supertasters—people who have many more taste buds than most people. About two-thirds of supertasters are females.

tannin—a natural chemical in the bark and leaves of many plants. The taste of tannin is present in many kinds of tea.

taste buds—taste-detecting cells located on little bumps (papillae) on the tongue, and also on other surfaces inside the mouth.

umami—a fifth taste—besides sweet, sour, salty, and bitter—that is detected by human taste buds. It is a savory, meatlike flavor of a chemical called glutamate.

uvula—the flap of flesh that dangles at the back of your mouth. It vibrates when you make an "aaahh" sound. There are taste buds on the uvula as well as the tongue and most other fleshy surfaces of your mouth.

Index

Page numbers for illustrations are in boldface.